Jack Bo...

Matchstick
Puzzles

OVER 200 OF THE WORLD'S MOST INCREDIBLE PUZZLES

Sterling Publishing Co., Inc.
New York

Library of Congress Cataloging-in-Publication Data Available

10 9 8 7 6 5 4 3 2

Published in 2006 by Sterling Publishing Co., Inc.
387 Park Avenue South, New York, NY 10016
© 2006 by Bookman International and Jack Botermans, Netherlands
Published in the English language by arrangement with Bookman International
B.V., Netherlands
Concept, text, design and photography by Jack Botermans, Netherlands
Edited by Carla van Splunteren and Heleen Tichler, Netherlands
Matchbox collection of P.A.G. Bakker, Netherlands
Distributed in Canada by Sterling Publishing
C/o Canadian Manda Group, 165 Dufferin Street,
Toronto, Ontario, Canada M6K 3H6
Distributed in the United Kingdom by GMC Distribution Services,
Castle Place, 166 High Street, Lewes, East Sussex, England BN7 1XU
Distributed in Australia by Capricorn Link (Australia) Pty. Ltd.
P.O. Box 704, Windsor, NSW 2756, Australia

Printed in China

Sterling ISBN-13: 978-1-4027-3699-5
          ISBN-10: 1-4027-3699-1

For information about custom editions, special sales, premium and
corporate purchases, please contact Sterling Special Sales
Department at 800-805-5489 or specialsales@sterlingpub.com.

America, c.1960.

"Let's play a game ..."

This is how it all started.

"We'll take a pile of matches and take turns removing one or two matches from the pile. The person who's left with the last match to pick up does the dishes." I did the dishes for the rest of the week. It was a good introduction to matchstick puzzles by my mother-in-law. Puzzles you will enjoy, I assure you. If there are children around, you might consider playing with burned matches, for safety reasons. Of course you can also use toothpicks.

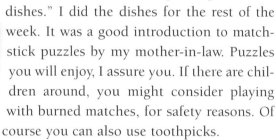

In my search for puzzles I met many collectors of matchbox covers and saw a lot of beautiful and interesting covers. The series shown in this book are from the collection of Piet Bakker (the Netherlands). They provide a nice distraction from all the cerebral activity you will need to solve the puzzles in this book. Have fun!

Jack Botermans

5

STRALSUNDER HOOGVLIEGER 30

STARGARDER SIDDERHALS 34

ENGELSE LANGVOORHOOFD-TUIMELAAR 36

HAMBURGER GETIJGERDE TUIMELAAR 18

NEURENBERGER BAGADET 19

WITGESCHUBDE MONNIKDUIF 8

Netherlands, c. 1960.

Some Suggestions

In many of the following puzzles you will be asked to find the correct number of squares, triangles and other shapes. To give you an idea of how to count them, we have two examples.

Figure A contains not only nine squares but also four big squares. In figure B you will find seven small squares and two big squares. It works the same way with equilateral triangles and rhomboids

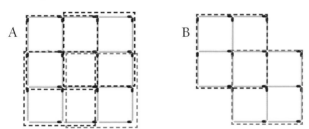

The squares, triangles and other shapes mentioned can have different sizes.

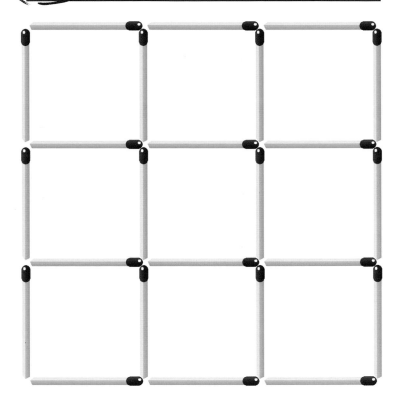

The First Six Puzzles

To warm up, here are six puzzles using the three-by-three grid shown on page 8.

1. Remove four matches and leave five squares.

2. Remove six matches and leave five squares.

3. Remove six matches and leave three squares.

4. Remove eight matches and leave four squares.

5. Remove eight matches and leave three squares.

6. Remove eight matches and leave two squares.

The Telegraph

A nice joke. Put match A on the table and put match B on top as indicated below; match C on top of B, D on top of C and so on. Match C and A have to be close to each other. Push on match E and the head of B will move up and down. You can make the telegraph as long as you like.

Italy, c. 1960.

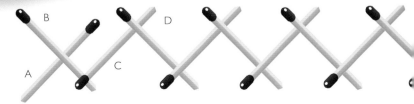

Nine Matches

With nine matches, can you make six triangles?

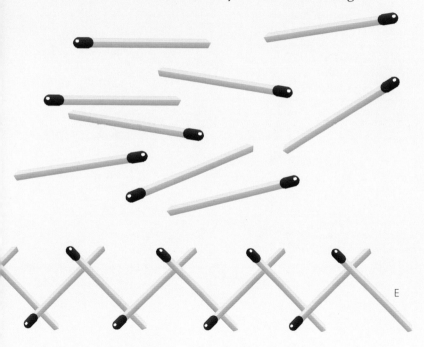

E

Eighteen Matches

Take 18 matches from this rectangle of 15 squares and leave three squares.

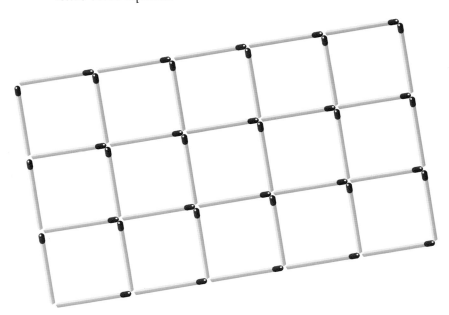

Southwest

Build this house with 10 matches. We see the house from the southwest angle. Now move only two matches to make us see the house from the northeast side.

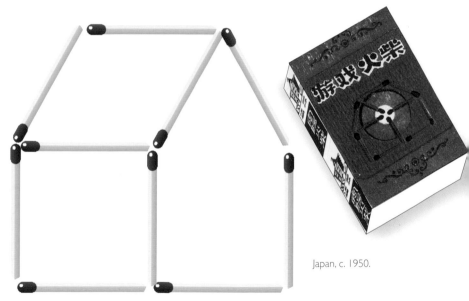

Japan, c. 1950.

America, c. 1930.

Strong Matchbox

Put the drawer of a match-box on top of the sleeve as shown on the left. Hit the top of the drawer with a full fist. Can you guess what happens?

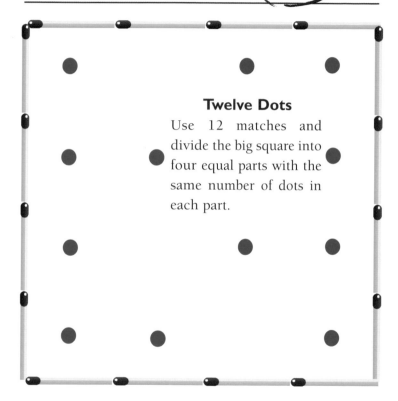

Twelve Dots

Use 12 matches and divide the big square into four equal parts with the same number of dots in each part.

Matchstick Magic

Transform the triangle into three connecting triangles
using the same number of matches.

Japan, c.1900.

Balancing Three

Arrange three matches into a triangle without having the match heads touching the table.

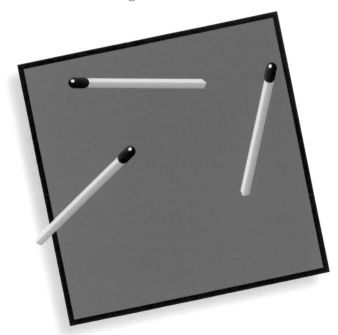

Double Question

Can you arrange 12 matches into three rows of 4 matches each and one row of 6 matches?

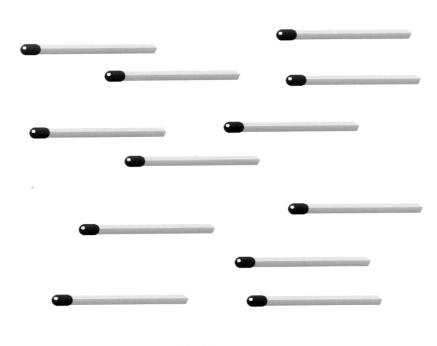

Only Five ...

Remove five matches from the figure below, in such a way
that the number of triangles is reduced to five.

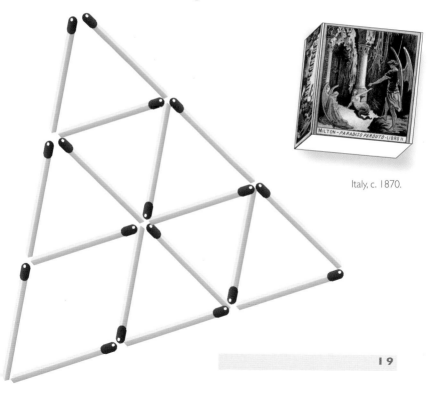

Italy, c. 1870.

19

From Twelve to Five ...

Three rows of four matches can be transformed into three times five...

Nuclear Problem

Take nine matches and arrange them so they form this nuclear sign. Now move only three matches to form three diamond shapes within the circle.

Austria, c. 1890.

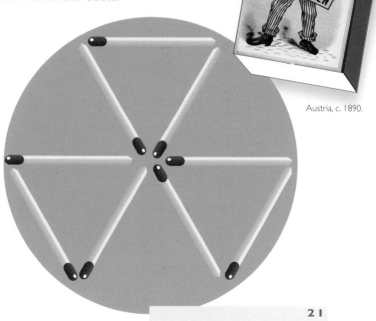

Six Matches

Arrange these six matches (without breaking them) into four equilateral triangles.

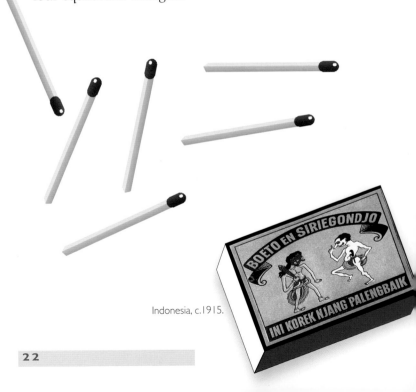

Indonesia, c.1915.

No Squares ...

The way they are arranged here, these 10 matches do not form one single square. Can you form two squares by moving only four matches?

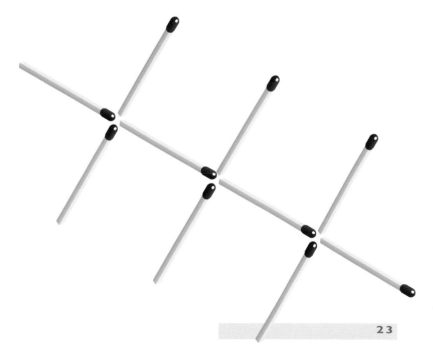

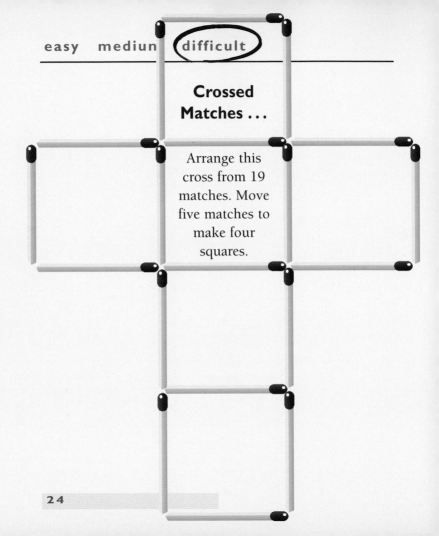

Crossed Matches . . .

Arrange this cross from 19 matches. Move five matches to make four squares.

Two Magic Squares

You need 12 matches to construct the figure below. We have two puzzles: **a.** Take away two matches and move six to create three equal squares. **b.** Take away two matches and move four to create three equal squares.

Four Squares

Make four squares with 16 matches. Can you make five squares of the same size with the same 16 matches?

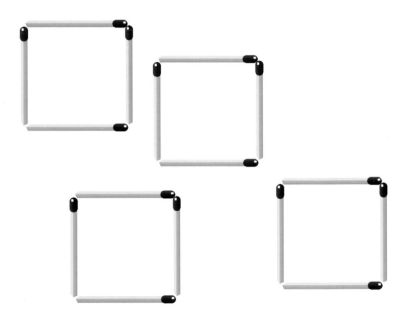

The Magic Bridge

Between these two boxes, can you construct a bridge covering the distance shown below, using only four matches?

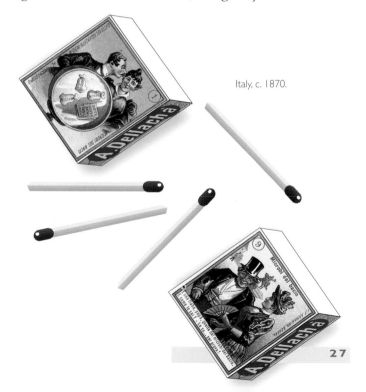

Italy, c. 1870.

The Curious Pig

By moving only two matches this pig suddenly becomes very inquisitive.

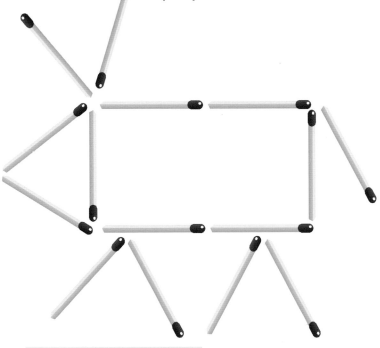

How to Build a House After Two Drinks

By moving six matches you can transform these two glasses into a house.

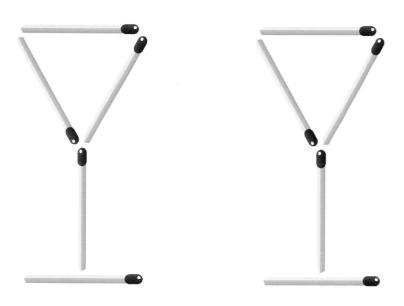

Greek Temple

Make 11 squares by moving only four matches.

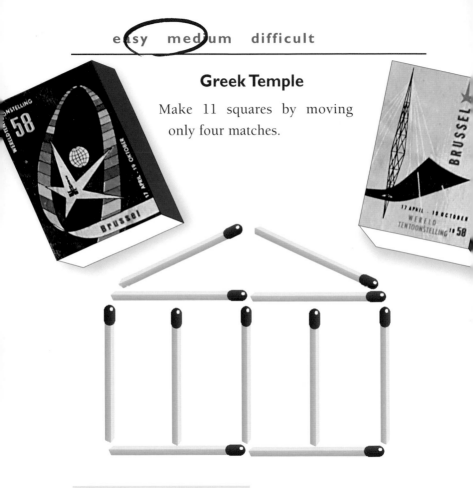

A Magic Brush?

Move two matches to sweep the coin onto the dustpan.

Belgium, Worldexpo 1958.

Hot Puzzle!

Put a glass over a coin. Support a match between this glass and another one next to it. Now remove the coin without allowing the match to fall.

Math

Change this fraction (⅙) to a unity by adding only one match.

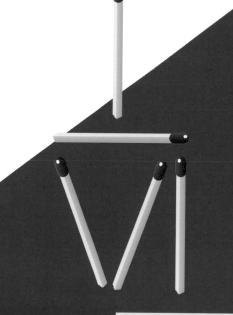

Hidden Square

Arrange four matches on the table as shown. Move one match and make a square.

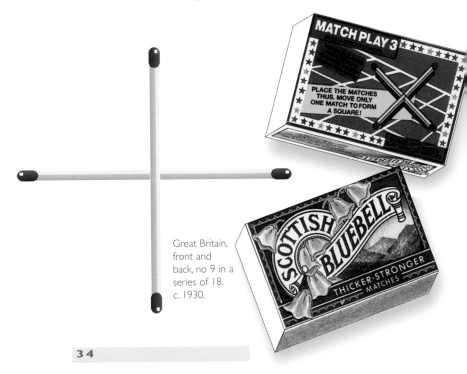

Great Britain, front and back, no 9 in a series of 18. c. 1930.

Three

Remove three matches so that you are left with three triangles.

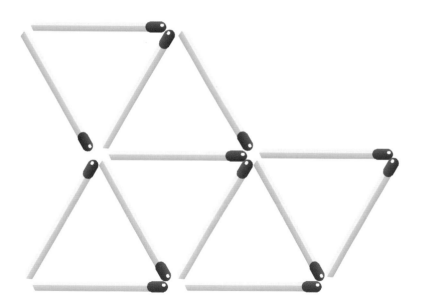

Hexagon

A. Move four matches to create three equilateral triangles.
B. Move four matches to create four equal rhomboids.

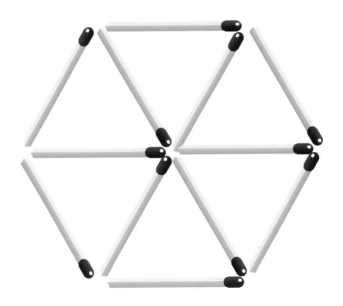

Just Two ...

Move two matches to create five equal squares.

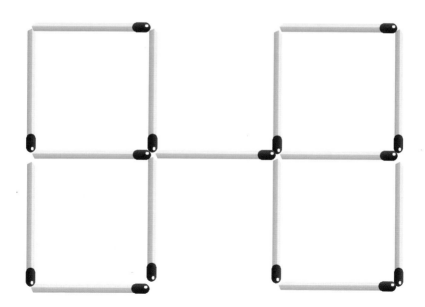

Step by Step

Remove six matches to create three equal squares.

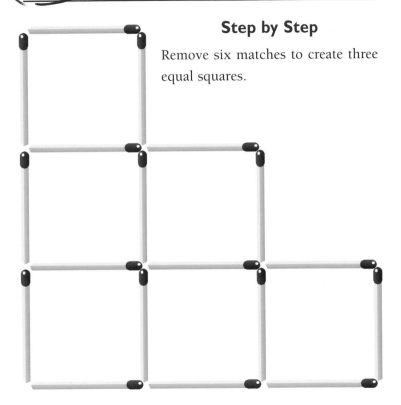

Tricky ...

With these eight matches make two squares and four equal triangles.

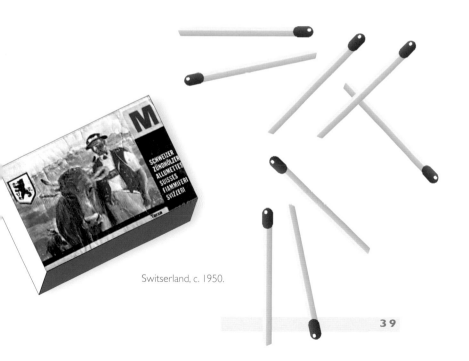

Switzerland, c. 1950.

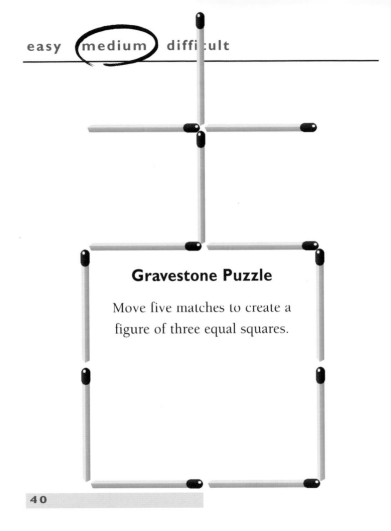

Gravestone Puzzle

Move five matches to create a
figure of three equal squares.

Three Squares

It is possible to create three equal squares with only six matches. Can you do it?

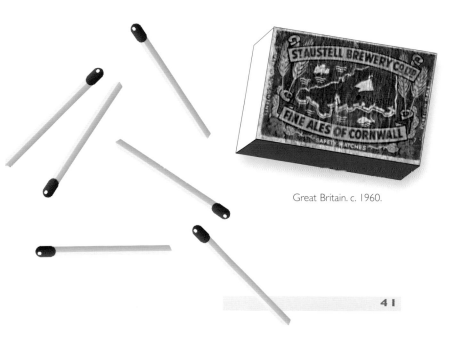

Great Britain. c. 1960.

Magic Four

Use four matches and a coin for this puzzle. Arrange them in such a way that neither the coin nor the match heads touch the table surface.

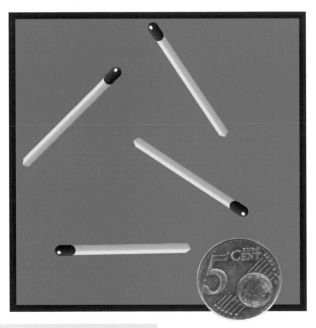

Equation

Move two matches to make the equation correct. There are three solutions.

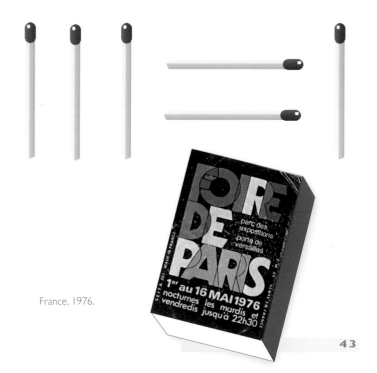

France, 1976.

Burning Question

Place two matches upright in the end of an empty match-box by sticking them between the sleeve and the drawer.

Balance a third match across the heads. Light this one in the middle. Which vertical match will catch fire first?

Romania,
Bucarest, 1969.

Minus Four Makes Four

Remove four matches so that you are left with four triangles of the same size.

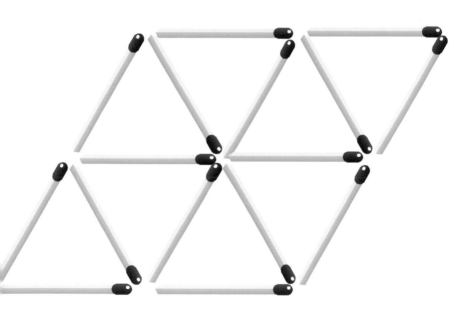

Bo Peep

Add three more matches to make two areas equal in shape and size.

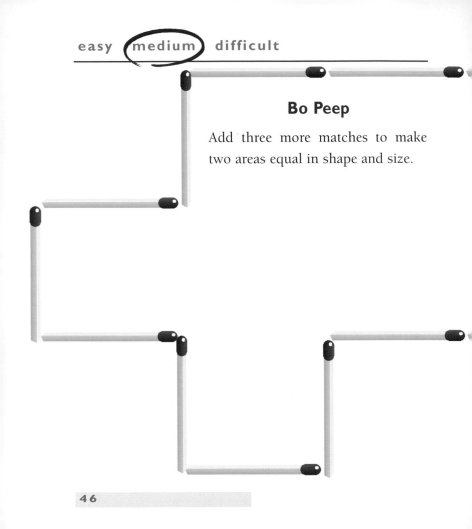

Northern Ireland, front and back, c. 1970.
The puzzle is shown on the back.
It came in a series of 18.

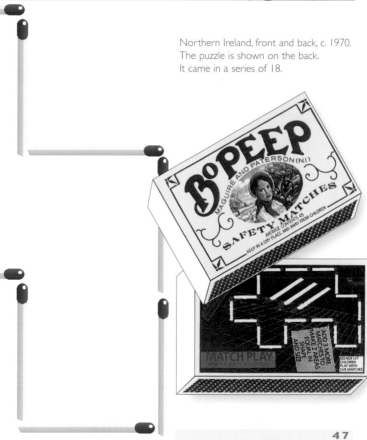

47

easy   medium   difficult

Five Sons

The big square is a farm. The smaller square is the homestead. The farmer wishes to retire but go on living at the homestead. He wants to divide the rest of the farm equally among his five sons. Can you do it for him?

Connections

Arrange six matches so that each touches the other five.

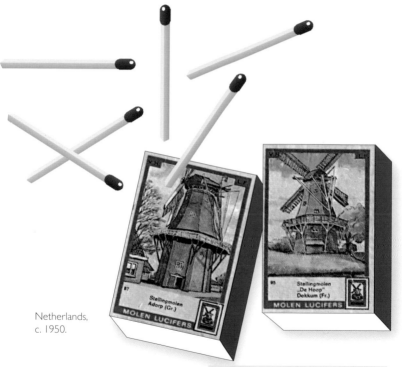

Netherlands,
c. 1950.

From 14 to 3

Remove two matches
so that you are
left with three
squares.

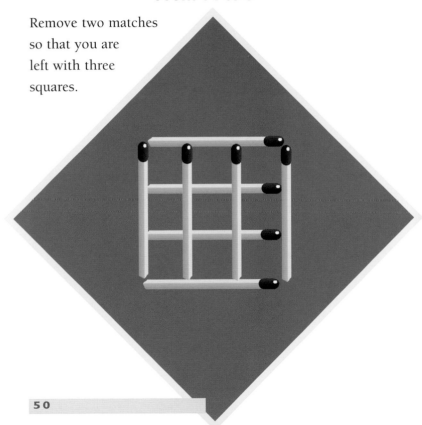

Cheating

Make one square from six matches.

Serious Puzzle?

Give someone six matches and ask her or him to lay them on the table so that they will make three-and-a-half dozen.

Sweden. Probably the most famous matchbox in Europe.

Pigsty

This figure made of 13 matches represents a pigsty with six equal compartments. But can you build a pigsty with 12 matches and still have six equal compartments?

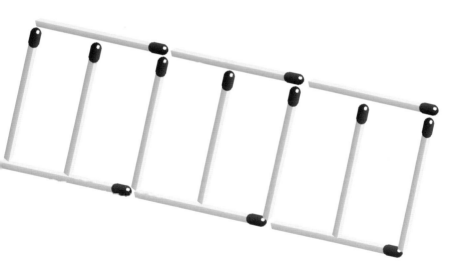

Match Magic 1

Lay down nine matches on the table and lift them all at the same time using only one more match.

America, c. 2000.

Mysterious Squares

A. Can you move only two matches and leave seven equal squares?

B. And remove only two matches from solution A and leave five equal squares?

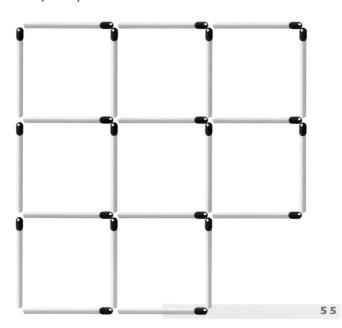

Jumping Matches 1

Arrange 15 matches in a row. You have to make five piles of three matches each, by moving one match at a time. The moving match has to jump over three matches at every move.

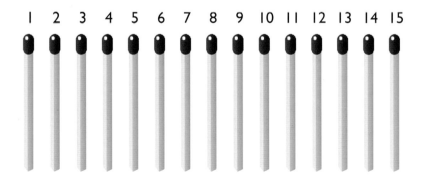

Greece, c. 1970.

The Untouchable Match

How can you remove the middle match out of the
center without touching it?

Seven Simple Solutions

Try to solve the next seven problems, using the figure shown here as a basis.

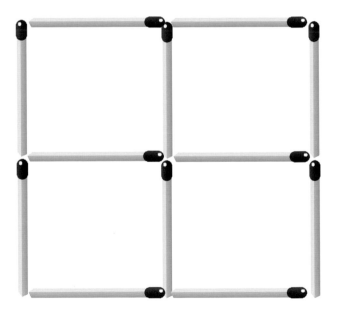

Number I

Remove one match and move four to make 11 squares.

Great Britain, c. 1960.

Number 2

Move four matches to be left with three squares.

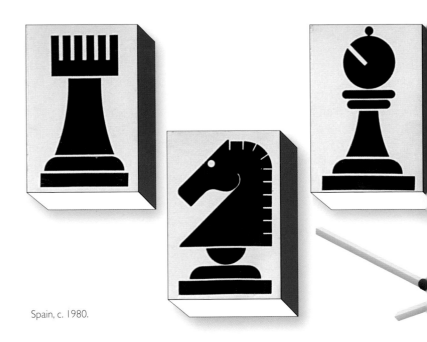

Spain, c. 1980.

Number 3

Move two matches to make seven squares.

Number 4

Move four matches to make 10 squares.

Greece, c. 1975.

Number 5

Remove three matches and move two to form three squares.

Number 6

Remove two matches so that two squares are left.

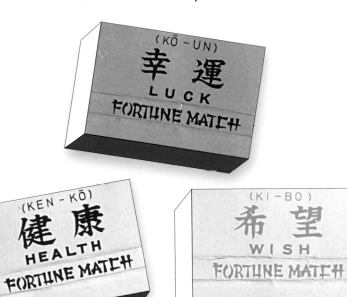

China, c. 1990.

Number 7

Move three matches so that three squares are left.

Impossible Moves

Arrange three matches in a row with the center match reversed pointing its head toward the player. The puzzle: pick up any two matches and reverse them, so that after three such reversals they are lined up with their heads pointing toward you. Although you can do it again and again, others will find it impossible to accomplish the correct moves.

Japan, c. 1950.

1   2   3

Without Four to Nine

Remove four matches so that nine squares are left.

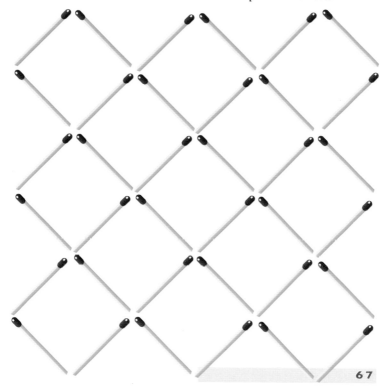

It Makes You Cry . . .

How can you turn this cross into a star without touching the four half-broken matches?

Drop-Load

Can you hold a box of matches vertically about 13 inches (33 cm) above the table and then let it drop so that it falls on its end and remains upright?

Netherlands, c 1960.

Match Point

There are 12 matches, four on each side. Can you move them into a square with five matches on each side?

Just Five . . .

Change this figure into four equal squares by removing 10 matches. There are five different solutions. Can you find them?

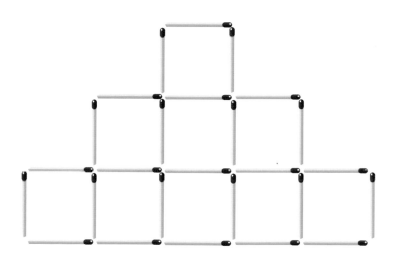

Swap Places

Put two pairs of coins, each pair in one color, between the matches. The colored coins should swap places. You can only move one coin at a time. It cannot go backward and it always has to go into an empty space, but it can jump over one occupied space. Can you swap the pairs of coins, beginning with a red one, in only eight moves?

Don't Move

Make this equation valid without moving, removing or adding a match. Can you do it?

Netherlands, c. 1960.

Deposit

Place four matches on a tablecloth as shown here. Put a coin in the center. This is our money box. Can you take the coin out of the box without touching it or the matches?

Fakir Matches

Can you put seven matches on the table without any of the heads touching the table surface?

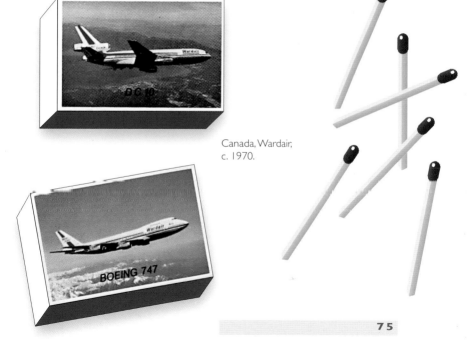

Canada, Wardair, c. 1970.

A Break

Just to train your nerves. Try to put as many matches as possible on an upright matchbox. How high can you get?

Great Britain, c. 1950.

Mysterious Behavior

Place a coin on a half-broken matchstick on top of a bottle. Can you move the coin into the bottle without touching coin, bottle, or matchstick?

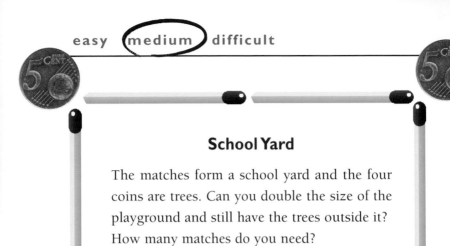

School Yard

The matches form a school yard and the four coins are trees. Can you double the size of the playground and still have the trees outside it? How many matches do you need?

Calculating Matches

The nine matches can be moved into (a) a vertical line of
12 or (b) a vertical line of 18.

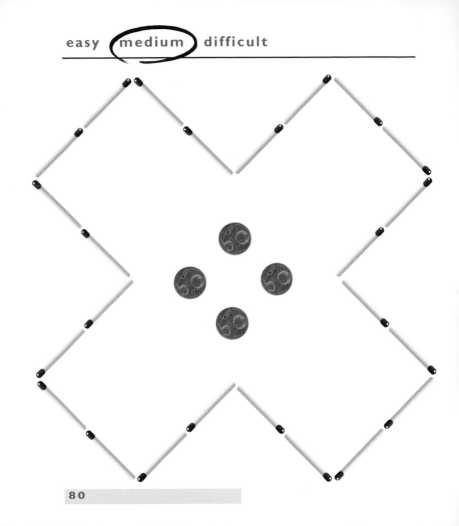

80

Crossed Matches

Divide the cross on page 74 into four equal parts with one coin each. How many matches do you need?

Dozens

How can you use ¾ dozen matches on the table to form three dozen?

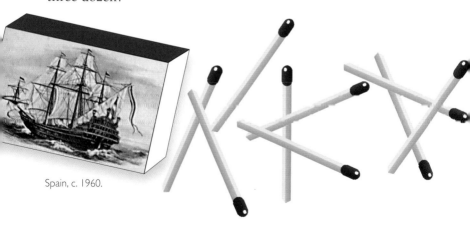

Spain, c. 1960.

To Square or Not to Square ...

Use 12 matches to make a figure that is not a square, but will form five squares after adding four matches.

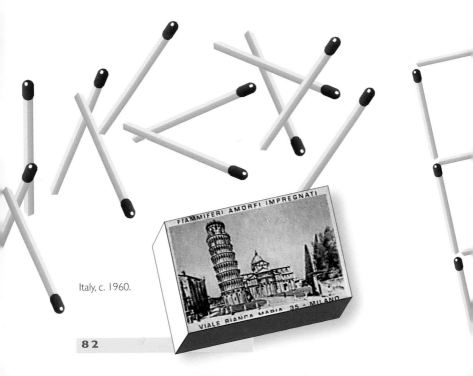

Italy, c. 1960.

From 15 to 9

Remove six matches to make
nine equal squares.

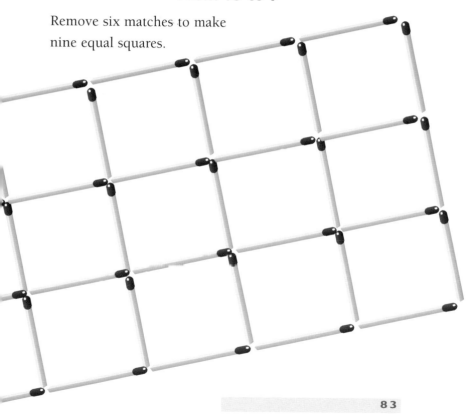

Six from Four

Can you arrange 12 matches in six rows so that each row contains four matches?

Finland, c. 1980.

France, 1970.

Just One!

Move one match and make this equation valid.

A Square Series—A

From 24 matches you can construct all kinds of squares. The following series will challenge you to make grids with a certain number of squares. Start by constructing four squares.

A Square Series—B

What about five squares?

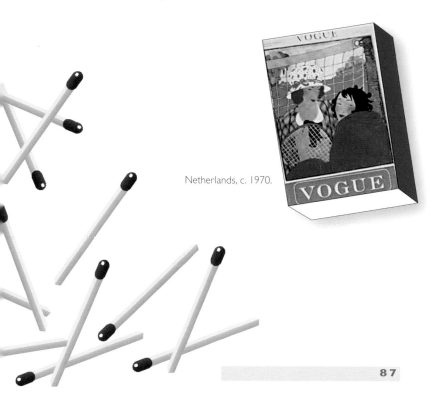

Netherlands, c. 1970.

easy (medium) difficult

A Square Series—C

And ever thought about six squares?

Netherlands, c. 1970.

A Square Series—D

This time, try seven squares.

A Square Series—E

What about nine squares?

Netherlands, c. 1965.

A Square Series—F

Still going strong? Now make 10 squares.

A Square Series—G

This is a true challenge: 14 squares out of 24 matches.

A Square Series—H

This could be killing. What about 42 squares?
Ever tried 110? (No solution provided!)
   Don't forget, only 24 matches!

Spain, c. 1970.

Match Magic 2

Start with 14 matches. Remove five from this pile. Now add three matches and have eight left.

Indonesia, c. 1980.

Proof

Can you prove the following equations by using matches?

9 - 3 = 4

11 - 3 = 6

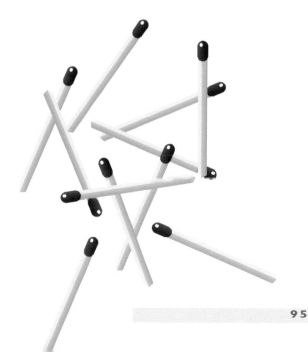

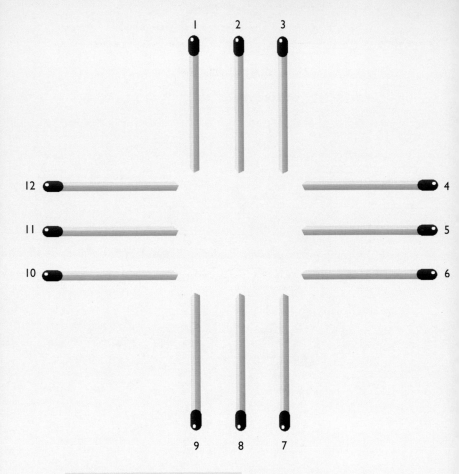

96

Jumping Matches 2

Move one match at a time. It is possible to finish with two matches on 1 to 6, by jumping over only two matches at a time. Can you do it?

Germany, c. 1970.

(A)maze Matches

By moving only four matches in the figure on page 99, can you make three squares?

Just a Way . . .

Can you put three-quarters of a dozen matches on the table, so that they show like three-and-a-half dozen? It is not allowed to break the matches in half.

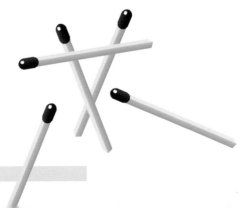

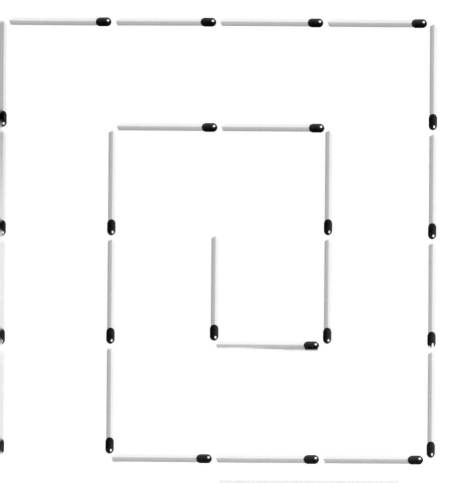

Match Star I

Add 12 matches and you can make 12 rhomboids without moving the other matches.

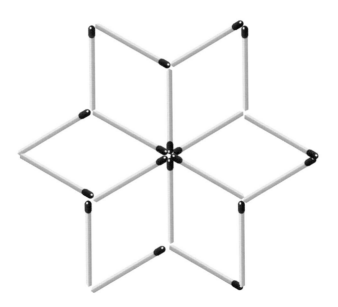

Match Star 2

From the figure on page 100, move four matches to make nine equilateral triangles.

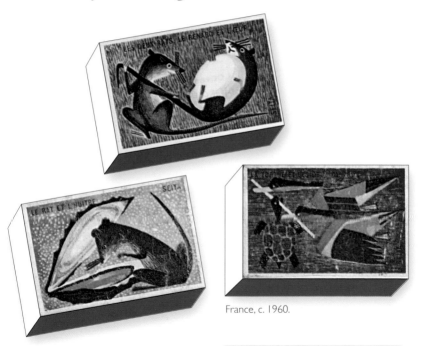

France, c. 1960.

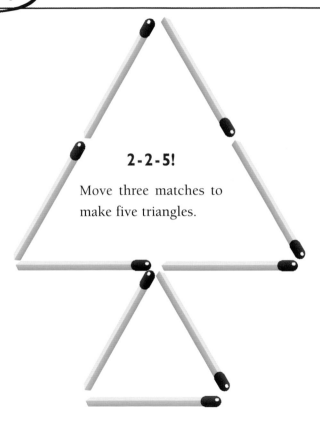

2-2-5!

Move three matches to
make five triangles.

3 - 2 = 4 + 1

Move two matches to make four triangles and one rhomboid.

Japan, c 1960.

103

Match Cube 1

Move two matches and create four triangles.

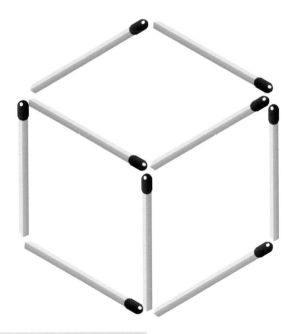

Match Cube 2

Using the figure on page 104 as a basis, create three triangles by moving only three matches.

Former Republic of Yugoslavia, c. 1960.

Floating Matches

Remove three matches from the ship-shaped figure and leave three triangles.

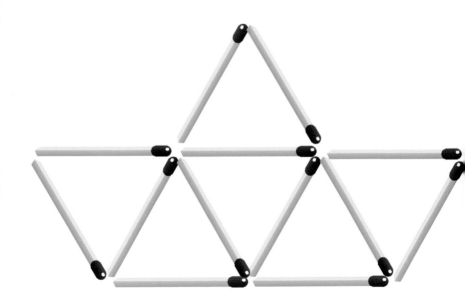

One out of Three

Move six matches and make five rhomboids.

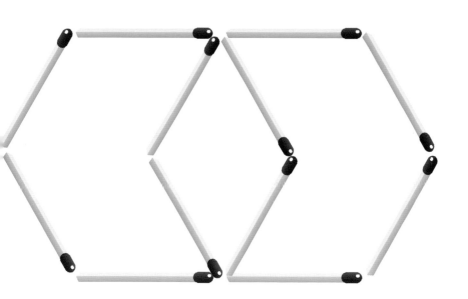

Two out of Three

Using the figure on page 107, move four matches and create four rhomboids.

Three out of Three

Using the figure on page 107, move four matches and create three rhomboids.

Japan, c. 1955.

Match Dice

Move four matches to create a cube.

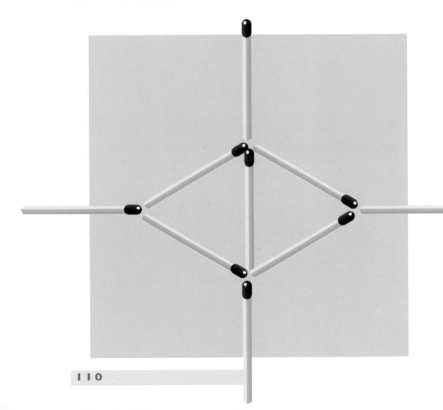

Only Four!

Move four matches to make six triangles.

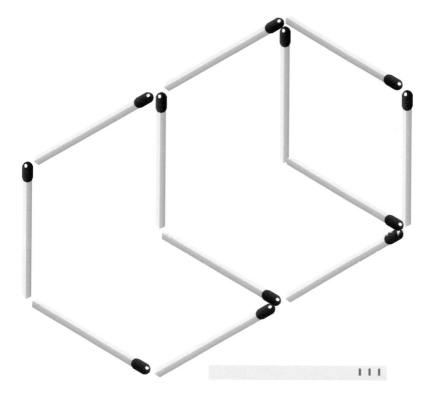

Magic Two

Move two matches to make two squares.

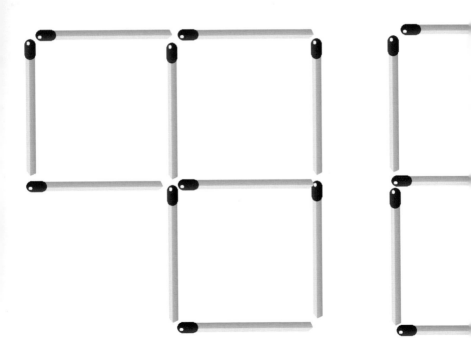

Magic Four

Move four matches to make five squares.

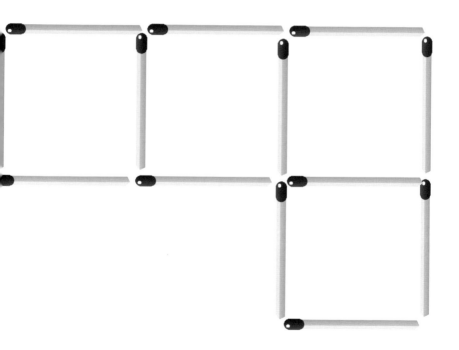

Square Problem

Make 11 squares with 15 matches.

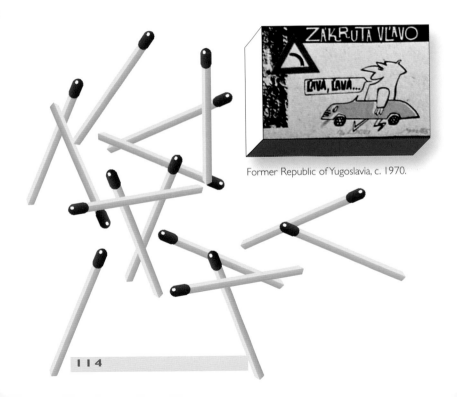

Former Republic of Yugoslavia, c. 1970.

114

Equation

Move one match and make this equation valid.

Luxemburg, c. 1960.

Magic Squares 1

Move two matches to make four equal squares.

Netherlands, 1952.

Magic Squares 2

Move two matches to make four squares—three small ones
and a big one.

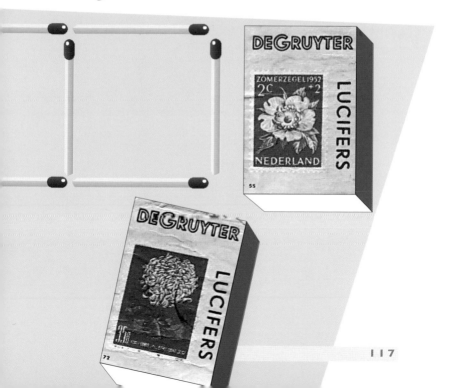

Clever

Move one match and make this equation valid.

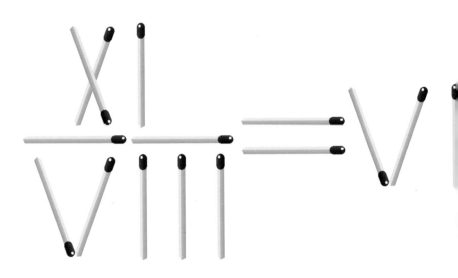

Four Equal Parts

Add eight more matches and divide the figure into four equal parts.

Hungaria, c. 1955.

119

71 Paul Mc. Cartney

73 Ringo Starr

61 George Harrison

80 John Lennon

Netherlands,
c. 1965.

The Magic Bridge

Can you make a bridge from the island in the center to the shore of the lake by using only two matches?

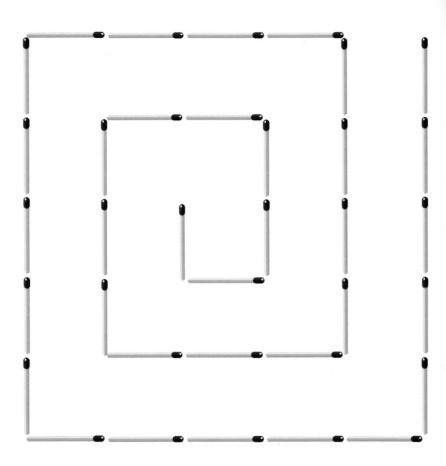

122

(A)mazing

Move only four matches in the figure on page 122 to make three squares.

India, c. 1950.

Solomon's Star

The star comprises eight triangles. Move two matches to reduce the number of triangles to six.

From Three 2 Five

Make five triangles by moving three matches.

Only Five

Move five matches and make four equal squares.

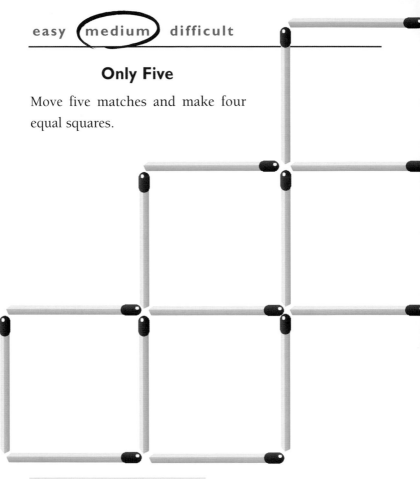

Magic Two

Move two matches in the figure on page
126 so that four squares are left.

Austria, c. 1960.

The Mysterious Eight I

Move eight matches in the figure on page 129 to make 13 squares.

Belgium, 1958.

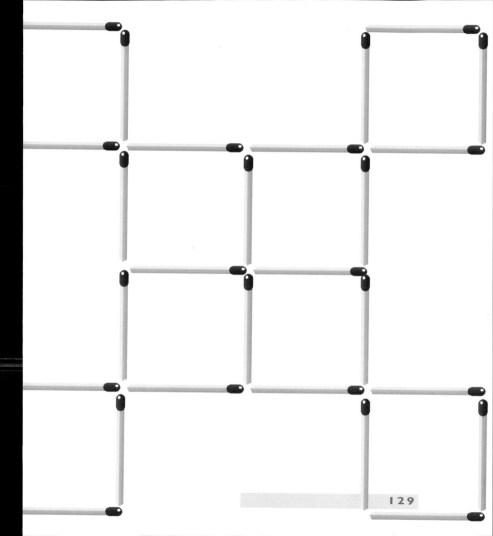

The Mysterious Eight 2

Move eight matches in the figure on page 129 and make six squares.

The Mysterious Eight 3

Again move eight matches in the figure on page 129, now to make nine squares.

Sweden, c. 1920.

The Mysterious Four I

Move only four matches in the figure on page 129 to make 10 squares.

Finland, c. 1960

difficult   medium   easy

The Mysterious Four 2

Again move four matches in the figure on page 129, now make seven squares.

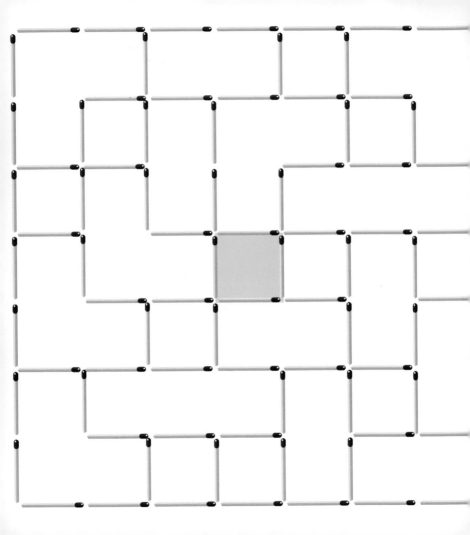

The 13 Hidden Matches

Remove 13 matches from the figure on page 134 so that 12 equal parts around the blue square in the center are left. This is a real brain twister.

Japan, c. 1950.

Square to Square

Move only two matches to make another square.

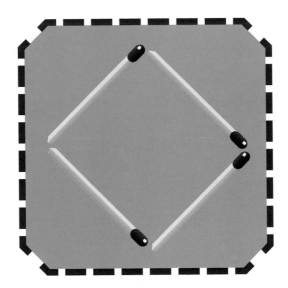

The Ladder

Move four matches to make four equal squares.

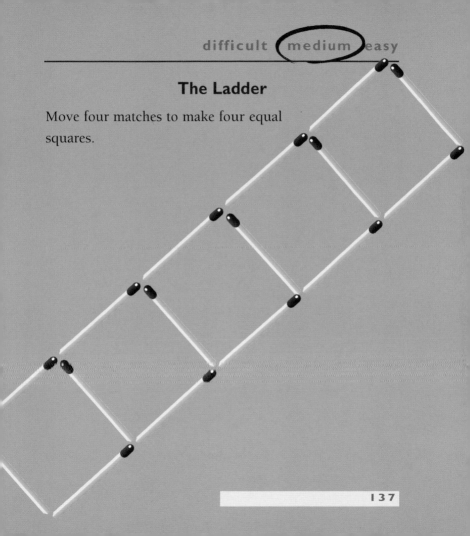

Many Squares

How many squares are hidden in this figure?

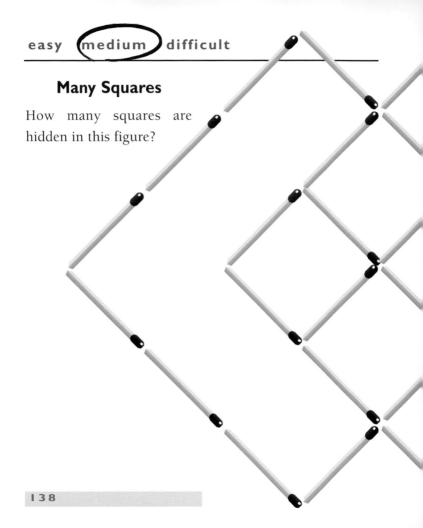

Just Four

Move only four matches
to make 10 squares.

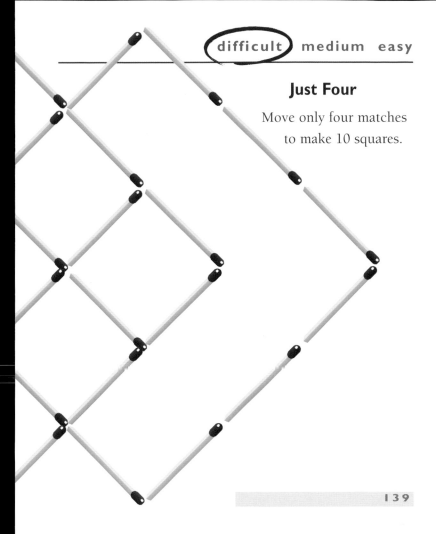

Triangular Problems I

Move two matches to make six triangles.

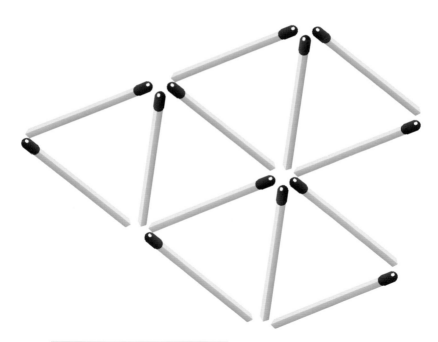

Triangular Problems 2

Remove one match from the figure on page 140 and then move two. You will make five rhomboids if you do it right.

Russia, c. 1960.

Triangular Problems 3

By removing one match and moving two in the figure on page 140, you can create two triangles and two rhomboids.

Russia, c. 1960.

Squary Squares

Move four matches to create two squares.

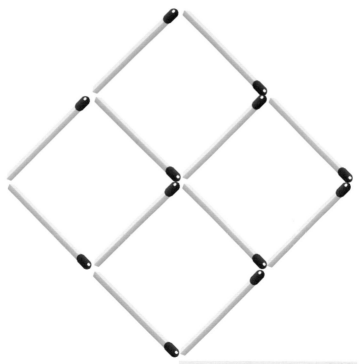

Math Again

Move one match and make the equation valid.

Russia, c. 1960.

Hot Problem

Move four matches to make 10 triangles.

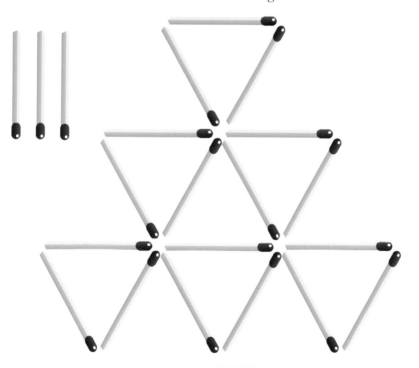

Box to Cabinet

Move only two matches to transform the box into a cabinet.

Twice As Big

Two four-sided spaces are made using 18 matches. One is twice as big as the other. Can you use 18 matches to make two five-sided spaces, one three times as big as the other?

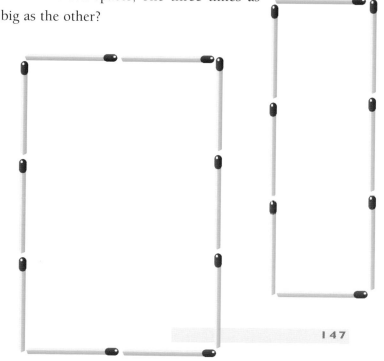

Bo-Peep

SAFETY
Match

MADE IN BELFAST BY
MAGUIRE & PATERSON
(N.I.) LTD.

BRITISH MADE

Stay at
an Anchor Hotel

COMPLETE TARIFF
OBTAINABLE FROM
17 CUMBERLAND AVENUE
LONDON, N.W.10

AVERAGE 38 MATCHES

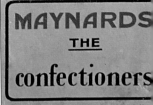

MAYNARDS
THE
confectioners

PUCK
MATCH
BRYANT & MAY LTD

BRITISH MADE

RUBY

MATCHES

THE
FRIENDLY
MATCH

MADE IN DUBLIN BY
MAGUIRE & PATERSON L

PROGRESSIVE
MATCHES

British & Proud of it !

Great Britain and Northern Ireland, c. 1960

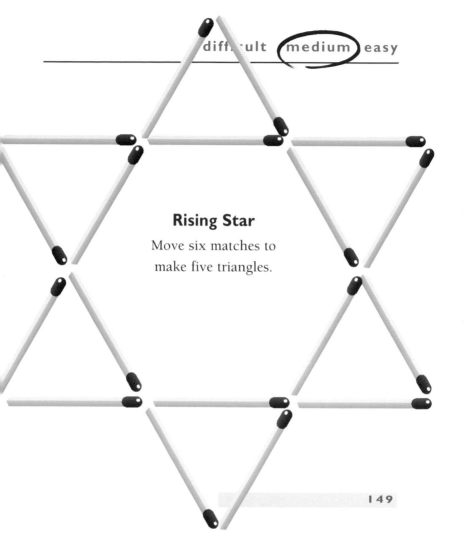

Rising Star

Move six matches to
make five triangles.

Boat Trip

A boat trip around Manhattan is carrying 20 passengers. Only 19 of them payed the fee. Now the captain wants to find the fare dodger by a counting system up to 19. Every last passenger takes a step backward. He lines the passengers up on the deck. The fare dodger can stand anywhere in the line (indicated by a match upside down). Where does the captain start counting to end up with the fare dodger?

One Square Less

Move five matches to make two squares.

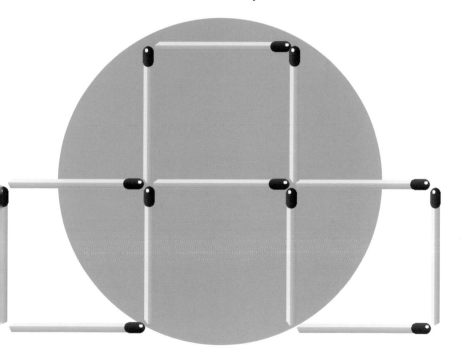

12 Matches

Can you make three identical rhomboids and two identical triangles with only 12 matches?

8 Matches

With eight matches, can you make a hexagonal shape with 90° corners?

Japan, c. 1950.

Shot Apple

Can you make a famous archer with only 10 matches?

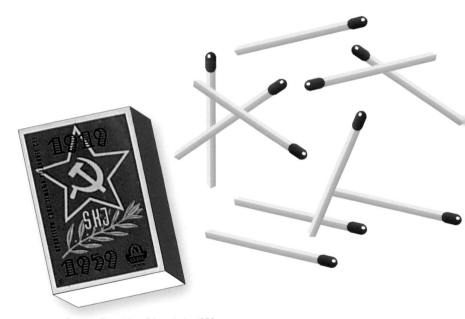

Former Republic of Yugoslavia, 1959.

Four Rhomboids

Move three matches to make four rhomboids.

Former Republic of Yugoslavia, 1959.

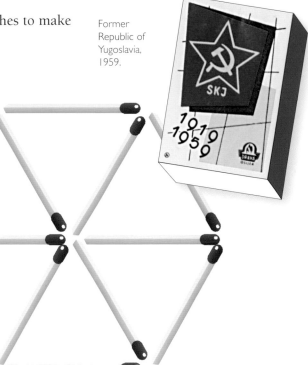

Magic Hexagon

Add one match and
move two to make two
rhomboids.

Former Republic of Yugoslavia, 1959.

156

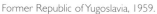
Former Republic of Yugoslavia, 1959.

Simple Equation

Move two matches to make the equation valid.

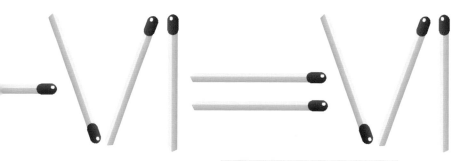

Chain Puzzle 1

Move four matches to make four squares.

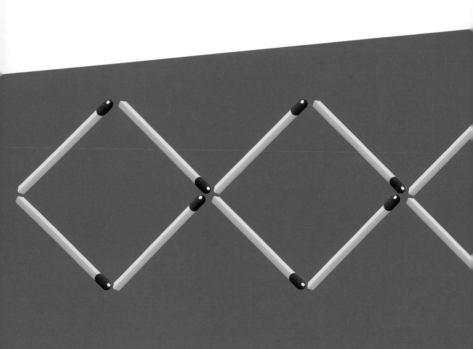

Chain Puzzle 2

Move four matches to make five squares.

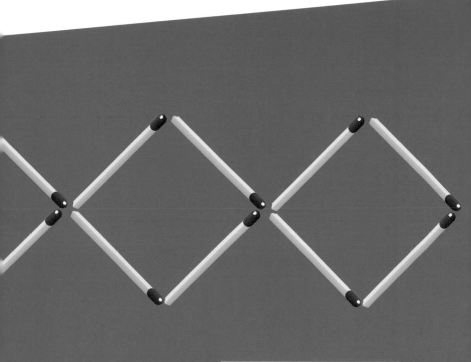

Chain Puzzle 3

Move four matches in the figure on pages 158–159 to make
six squares.

Chain Puzzle 4

Move four matches in the figure on pages 158–159 to make seven squares.

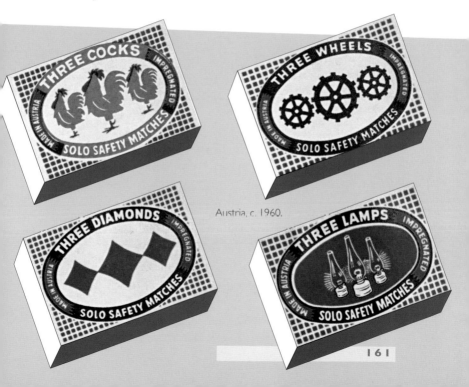

Austria, c. 1960.

(A)maze

Move two matches to make two squares.

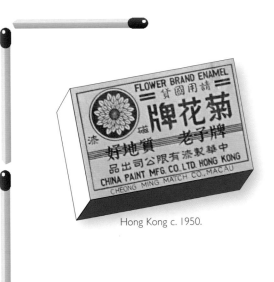

Hong Kong c. 1950.

162

Trivial?

Can you make a
square with two
matches without
breaking or bending
them?

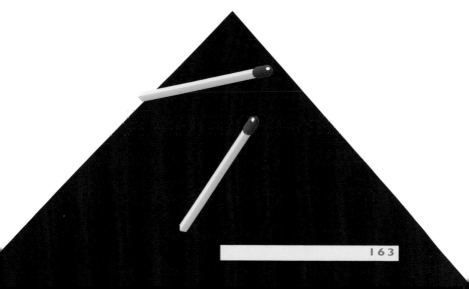

163

Only Four

Move four matches to make a hexagon and six equal triangles.

Zigzag Puzzle

Move four matches to make two squares.

Stars and . . .

Move six matches to make a six-pointed star.

Missing Match

Move one match to arrange six matches in a row, both horizontally and vertically.

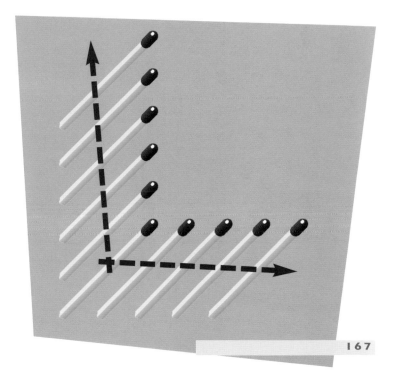

Surprising Four

Move only four matches to make 18 triangles.

Afghanistan, c. 1950.

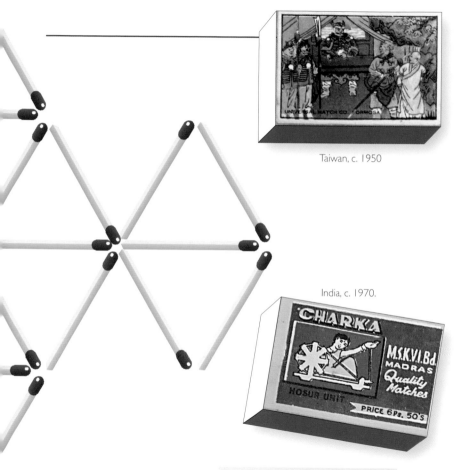

Taiwan, c. 1950

India, c. 1970.

Match Science!

How many matchboxes of 58 x 38 x 20 mm fit into one cubic meter?

Match Science 2

How many matches do you need to cover the distance between the earth and the moon?

Japan, c. 1930.

Match Science 3

How many matches can you make out of a piece of wood of 10 x 1 x 1 m?

Match Science 4

How much time do you need to count 1,000,000,000 matches when you count three per second?

Belgium, c. 1980.

173

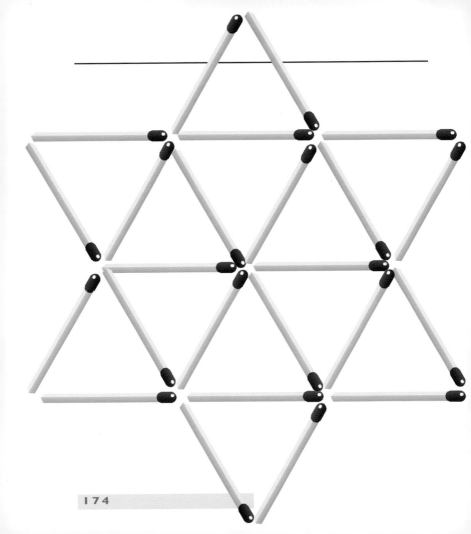

Stars in Heaven

1. How many triangles can you find in the star on page 174?

2. Now move six matches to make nine triangles plus one hexagon.

Former Republic of Yugoslavia, c. 1960.

Exciting Equation

Move one match and make the equation valid.

Netherlands, c. 1960.

Equal Squares

Remove three matches from this figure of eight equal squares to make a new figure with eight equal squares.

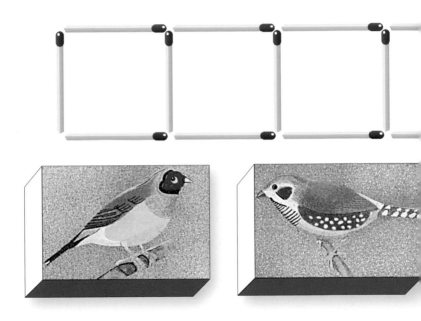

Equal Shapes

Remove nine matches to make a figure with nine equal shapes and the coin in the middle.

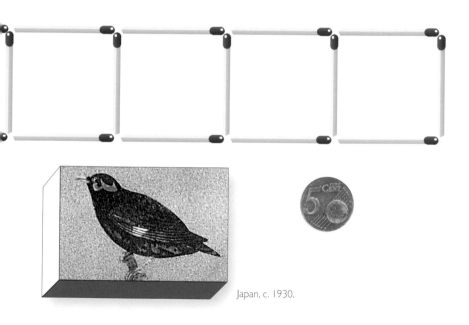

Japan, c. 1930.

India, c.1950

Solutions

Page 8. **The First Six Puzzles**

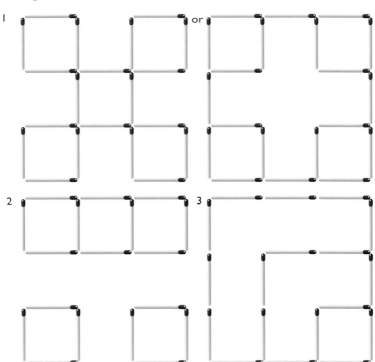

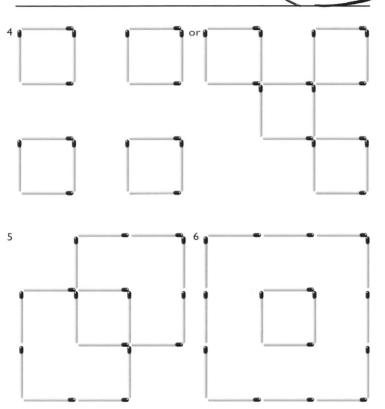

4

or

5

6

Solutions

Page 11. **Nine Matches**

Page 12. **Eighteen Matches**

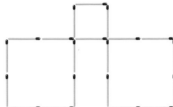

Page 13. **Southwest**

Page 15. **Twelve Dots**

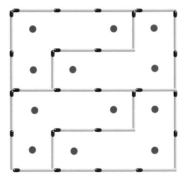

Page 14. **Strong Matchbox**
The box "jumps away" and stays in its original condition.

Page 16. **Matchstick Magic**

Page 17. **Balancing Three**

Page 18. **Double Question**
One diagonal consists of six matches, the rows each consist of four matches.

Page 19. **Only Five...**

Solutions

Page 20. **From Twelve to Five...**

Page 21. **Nuclear Problem**

Page 22. **Six Matches**

Page 23. **No Squares...**

Page 25. **Two Magic Squares**

Page 24. **Crossed Matches...**

Page 26. **Four Squares**

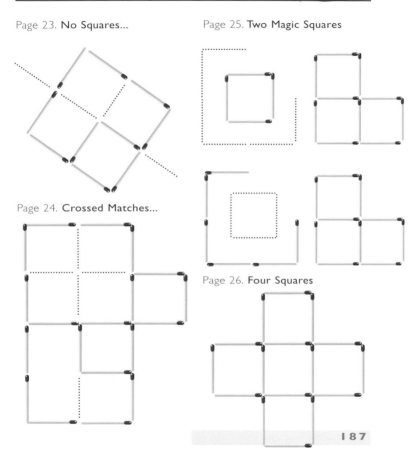

Solutions

Page 27. **The Magic Bridge**

Page 28. **The Curious Pig**

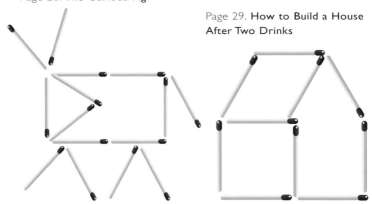

Page 29. **How to Build a House After Two Drinks**

Page 30. **Greek Temple**

Page 32. **Hot Puzzle!**
Light the match with another match and quickly blow it out. The head will stick to the glass so that you can pick up the glass and remove the coin.

Page 31. **A Magic Brush?**

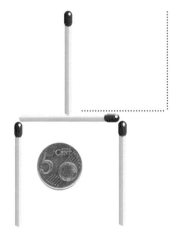

Page 33. **Math**

Solutions

Page 34. **Hidden Square**

Page 36. **Hexagon**

A

Page 35. **Three!**

B

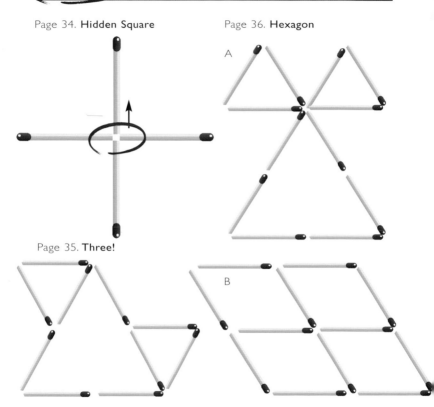

Solutions

Page 37. Just Two...

Page 39. Tricky...

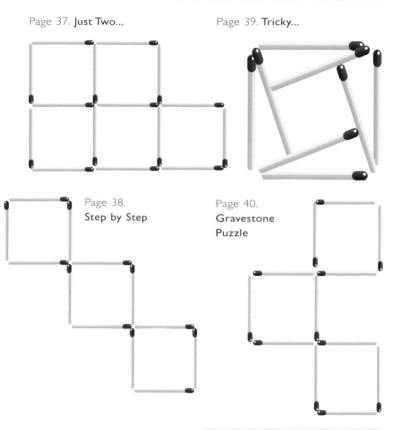

Page 38.
Step by Step

Page 40.
Gravestone
Puzzle

191

Solutions

Page 41. **Three Squares**

Page 42. **Magic Four**

Page 43. **Equation**

1

2

3

$$|^1 = |^1$$

Page 44. **Burning Question**
Neither will. The center match
will burn for a minute and then
fall off.

Page 45. **Minus Four Makes Four**

Page 48. **Five Sons**

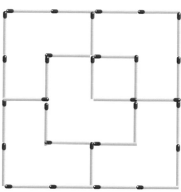

Page 46-47. **Bo Peep**
See the upper-left corner of
the box.

Page 49. **Connections**

Solutions

Page 50. **From 14 to 3**

Page 52. **Serious Puzzle?**

Page 53. **Pigsty**

Page 51. **Cheating**

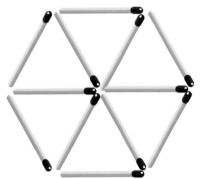

Page 54. **Match Magic 1**

Lay the matches down as shown in the figure and lift all the matches with the match at the bottom.

Page 55. **Mysterious Squares**

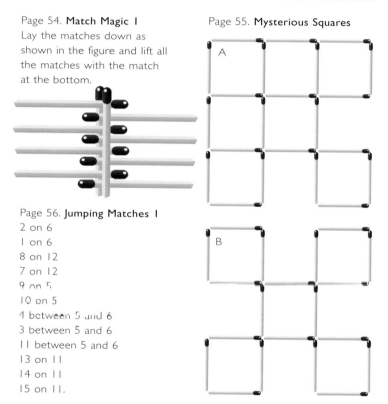

Page 56. **Jumping Matches 1**

2 on 6
1 on 6
8 on 12
7 on 12
9 on 5
10 on 5
4 between 5 and 6
3 between 5 and 6
11 between 5 and 6
13 on 11
14 on 11
15 on 11.

Solutions

Page 57. **The Untouchable Match**
Move the left match to the right side and the center match will not be in the center anymore.

Page 58. **Seven Simple Solutions—Number 1**

Page 60. **Seven Simple Solutions—Number 2**

Page 61. **Seven Simple Solutions—Number 3**

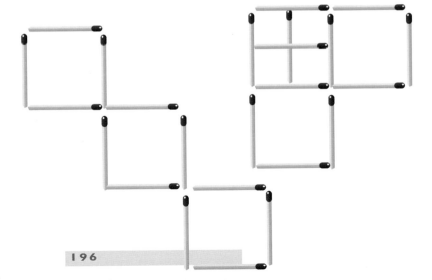

Page 62. **Seven Simple Solutions—Number 4**

Page 64. **Seven Simple Solutions—Number 6**

Page 63. **Seven Simple Solutions—Number 5**

Page 65. **Seven Simple Solutions—Number 7**

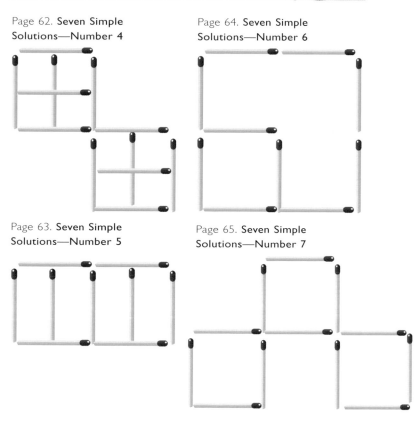

Page 66. Impossible Moves

This is one of several solutions:
1 and 2, 1 and 3, 1 and 2. The secret is to reverse the outer matches when you give the problem to someone else. The heads of the outer matches should point toward him and the center match should point away. The trick will be impossible to do.

Page 68. It Makes You Cry...

Put a drop of water in the center and a four-pointed star will form.

Page 69. Drop-Load

Before you drop it, see to it that the drawer projects slightly at the upper end, but keep this concealed with your hand. When you drop the box, the force of the drawer sliding into place will cause the box to remain upright.

Page 70. Match Point

Page 67. Without Four to Nine

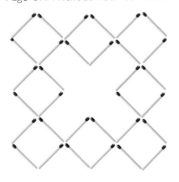

Page 71. **Just Five...**

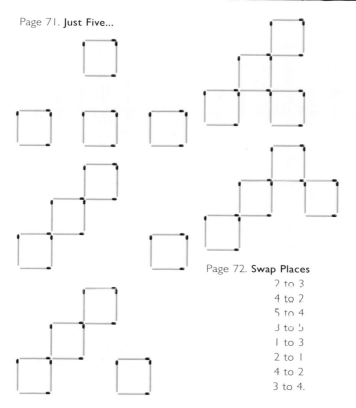

Page 72. **Swap Places**

2 to 3
4 to 2
5 to 4
3 to 5
1 to 3
2 to 1
4 to 2
3 to 4.

Page 73. **Don't Move**
Read it upside down.

Page 74. **Deposit**
Start scratching the tablecloth with your fingernail on the bottom side of the figure. The coin will appear slowly from under the match.

Page 75. **Fakir Matches**

Page 77. **Mysterious Behavior**
Drop two drops of water on the knick of the match. It will stretch after a while and the coin will fall into the bottle.

Page 78. **School Yard**

Page 79. **Calculating Matches**

Page 80. **Crossed Matches**

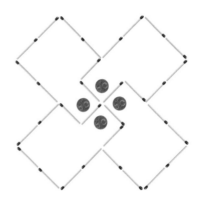

Page 82. **To Square or Not to Square**

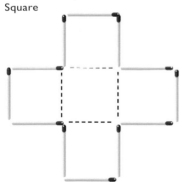

Page 81. **Dozens**

Solutions

Page 83. **From 15 to 9**

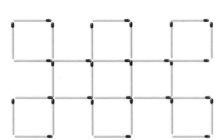

Page 85. **Just One!**

Page 84. **Six from Four**

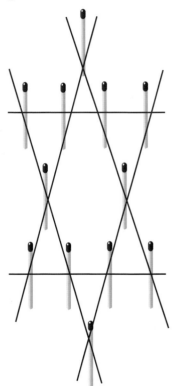

202

Page 86. **A Square Series—A**

Page 88. **A Square Series—C**

Page 87. **A Square Series—B**

Page 89. **A Square Series—D**   Page 91. **A Square Series—F**

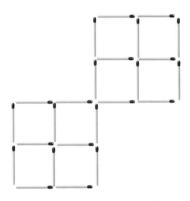

Page 90. **A Square Series—E**   Page 92. **A Square Series—G**

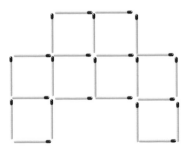
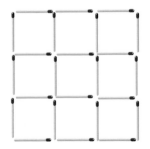

Page 93. **A Square Series—H**

Page 95. **Proof**

Page 94. **Match Magic 2**
The three matches added are of
course added to the five
removed matches.

Page 96–97. **Jumping Matches 2**
7 on 4, 12 on 3, 9 on 1, 11 on 6,
10 on 2, 8 on 5.

Solutions

Page 98. **(A)maze Matches**

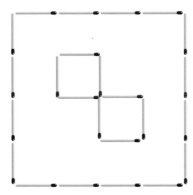

Page 100. **Match Star 1**

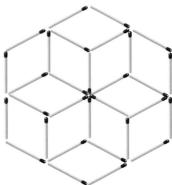

Page 98. **Just a Way...**
Place a pile of three and a pile of six matches next to each other on the table. Now you will have three-and-a-half dozen matches.

Page 101. **Match Star 2**

Page 102. **2-2-5**

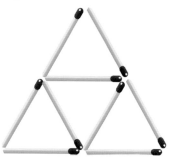

Page 103. **3-2=4+1**

Page 104. **Match Cube 1**

Page 105. **Match Cube 2**

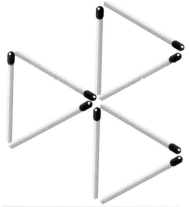

Page 106. **Floating Matches**

Page 108. **Two out of Three**

Page 107. **One out of Three**

Page 109. **Three out of Three**

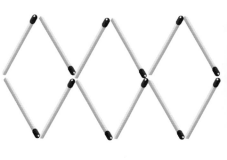

Solutions

Page 110. **Match Dice**

Page 112. **Magic Two**

Page 111. **Only Four!**

Page 113. **Magic Four**

209

Page 114. **Square Problem**

Page 116. **Magic Squares 1**

Page 117. **Magic Squares 2**

Page 115. **Equation**

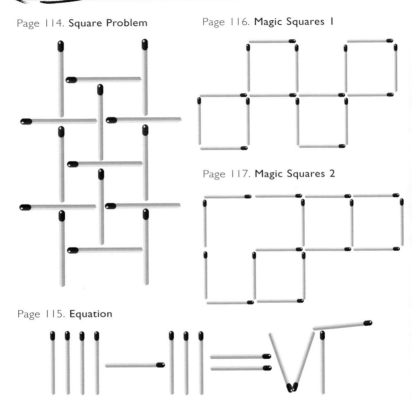

Page 118. **Clever**

40/8=5

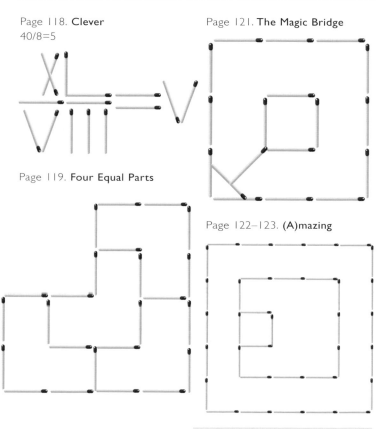

Page 119. **Four Equal Parts**

Page 121. **The Magic Bridge**

Page 122–123. **(A)mazing**

Solutions

Page 124. **Solomon's Star**

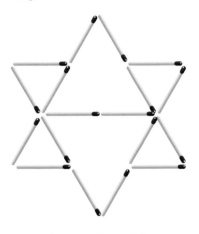

Page 126. **Only Five**

Page 127. **Magic Two**

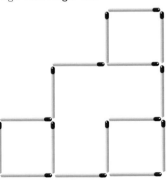

Page 125. **From Three 2 Five**

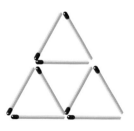

Page 128–129. **The Mysterious Eight 1**

Page 130. **The Mysterious Eight 2**

Page 131. **The Mysterious Eight 3**

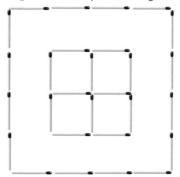

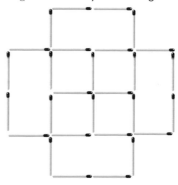

Page 132. **The Mysterious Four 1**

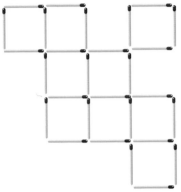

Page 133. **The Mysterious Four 2**

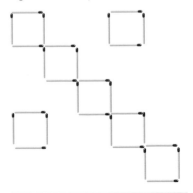

Page 134–135. **The 13 Hidden Matches**

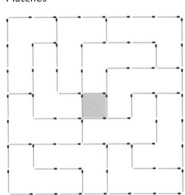

Page 136. **Square to Square**

Page 137. **The Ladder**

Page 140. **Triangular Problems I**

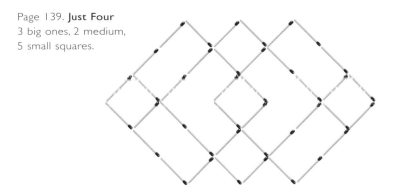

Page 138. **Many Squares**
16 squares. 3 big ones, 4 medium
(in the centre square), and
9 small squares in the center.

Page 139. **Just Four**
3 big ones, 2 medium,
5 small squares.

Solutions

Page 141. **Triangular Problems 2**   Page 143. **Squary Squares**

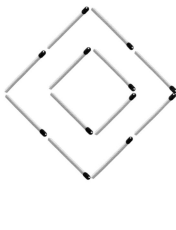

Page 142. **Triangular Problems 3**

Page 144. **Math Again**

Solutions

Page 145. **Hot Problem**

Page 146. **Box to Cabinet**

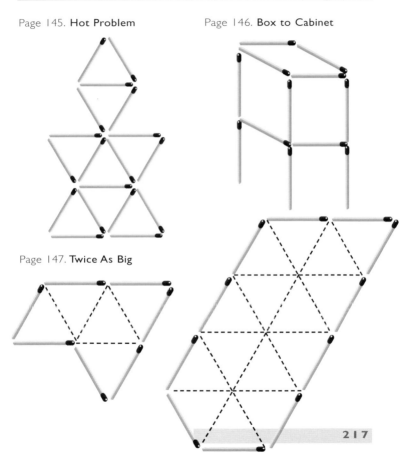

Page 147. **Twice As Big**

Solutions

Page 149.
Rising Star

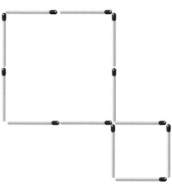

Page 150. **Boat Trip**
The captain starts with the passenger who is two places ahead of the fare dodger.

Page 151. **One Square Less**

Page 152. **12 Matches**

Page 153. **8 Matches**

Page 154. **Shot Apple**

Page 155. **Four Rhomboids**

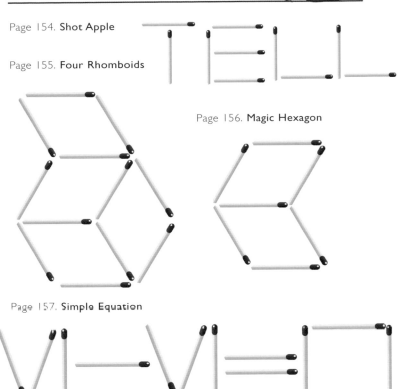

Page 156. **Magic Hexagon**

Page 157. **Simple Equation**

Solutions

Page 158–159. **Chain Puzzle 1**

Page 158–159. **Chain Puzzle 2**

Page 160. **Chain Puzzle 3**

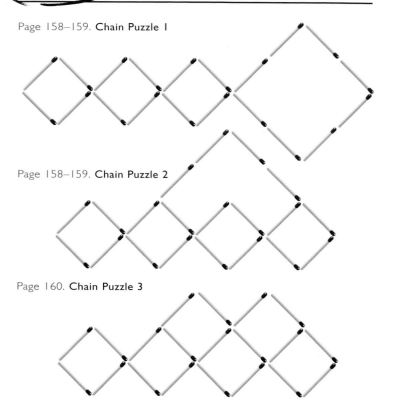

Page 161. **Chain Puzzle 4**

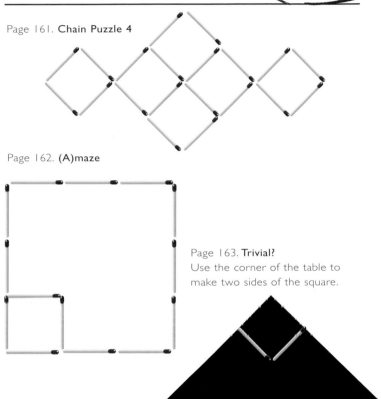

Page 162. **(A)maze**

Page 163. **Trivial?**
Use the corner of the table to
make two sides of the square.

Solutions

Page 164. **Only Four**

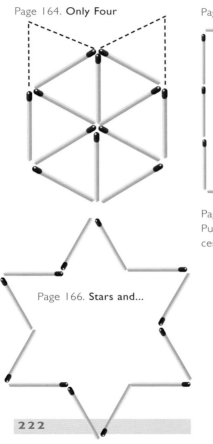

Page 165. **Zigzag Puzzle**

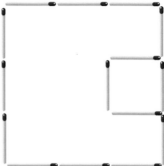

Page 167. **Missing Match**
Put the top match on the center match.

Page 166. **Stars and...**

222

Page 168–169.
Surprising Four
14 small ones and
four big ones.

Page 170. **Match
Science 1**
22,686 matchboxes.

Page 171. **Match Science 2**
7,500,000,000 matches.

Page 172. **Match Science 3**
50,000,000 matches.

Page 173. **Match Science 4**
10,561 years and 219 days.

Page 174–175. **Stars in Heaven**
1. 20 triangles. 12 small ones,
six medium and two big ones.
2. See picture on the right.

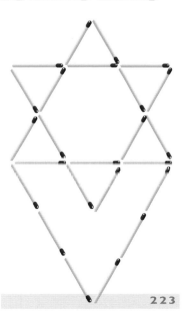

Solutions

Page 176–177. **Exciting Equation**

Page 178. **Equal Squares**

Page 179. **Equal Shapes**

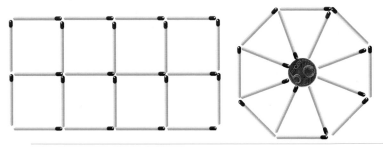